Poetry in Commotion

Jodie Danner

BookLeaf Publishing
India | USA | UK

Presentation by *BookLeaf Publishing*

Web: www.bookleafpub.com

E-mail: info@bookleafpub.com

ISBN: 9789358736724

First edition 2023

I'm dedicating this collection to Niamh and Esmé, my wonderful Daughters. Both so different, both so incredible and both so loved.

ACKNOWLEDGEMENT

I would like to thank my Husband, Neil, Mum Denise, Dad Jimmy, Stepdad John my Mother in Law Joan, Daughters Niamh and Esmé, Sister and Brother, Gemma and Dean for always being my biggest supporters.

Also my wonderful friends Debbie, Sandra, Mark, Alison and Jane who navigated me through a difficult year with kindness and love.

My coach Tom for always believing in me even when and especially when I didn't believe in myself.

My amazing circle Sian, Becky, Emma, Stella, Yvonne and Laura who have shown me how friendship can be with good people.

PREFACE

I started to write the content for this collection when I gave birth to my youngest child. It was initially an outpouring of worry, angst but eventually gave way to appreciation and acknowledgement of the human condition. The importance of feeling the uncomfortable feelings along with the happiness.

By writing my feelings down I found myself able to navigate difficult friendships and really analyse the plethora of friendships that I have and how they shape me.

Poetry in Commotion is exactly that.

An untangling of the chaos into something more fathomable on paper.

Esmé

There was a girl who was night and day
A blooming snowdrop to a barren clearing
A burst of colour that fades to grey
A breathtaking breeze to a heat that's searing.

A precious pearl that looks fragile to hold
But is housed in a bulletproof case
A delicate parchment that will just not fold
A resilience behind a youthful face.

This energy will have to be understood and
steered
To make sure it is used for good.
Right now, I have to show her that she is not
feared.
I'm not backing down when I usually would.

One day I'm sure she will move mountains with
ease
Be unafraid to challenge a wrong
For now I'm just having to match her unfazed
And show her that her mum is as strong

Lockdown Lunacy

Scrolling some old pictures tonight
And came across this and shuddered.
Such weird practices we participated in
During a time that was so unruddered.

Display your rainbows, stay safe, stay home
Drilled into us on a loop
When the so called government brazenly ducked
right under their own hoop.

For a while I played the game
But witnessed every day
How early years children were being
Damaged every single day

Years of time lost out on with relatives
Family dying all alone
Meanwhile in Downing st the cheese and the
wine
We're setting the rebellious tone.

I hope there is some recompense
For the time that was wasted and lost.
The coldest of hours touching hands
Through windows covered in frost.

Call me anti-vax, call me a fool
Call me anything and everything you can.
I'll never forgive the time that was lost,
I never banged a single pan.

Doubt Wrestling

It's cold it's wet, work tired me out,
I may just give it a miss.
But as I toy with the idea of a night of rest, I try
to tell myself this....

Two years ago the thought of grappling would
have me gripped with fear,
It would have taken more than a stern self word
to drag my nervous arse here.

It's ok to be new and not know what to do
So long as you're open to learning
Soon enough things start to fall into place,
Those reluctant cogs start turning.

So after the sessions where I feel I'm the nail,
I look at this feeling this way.
I'm still on the right path in the journey I'm on,
You must be stopped to be shown the right way.

So while sometimes my curve may seem
arduous and long,
for this stubborn old Jodie Danner
At least I'm submitting those still on the couch
And I'm in class with the finest of hammers.

Are you happy?

I was asked today "are you happy in life?"
A question so heavy and deep.
I paused as I wondered how I could answer such
a thing
And what personal truths I would keep.

I've been blessed with two girls, a husband a
home.
Two dogs, a family I adore.
When it comes to my personal satisfaction
I can't lie....I want to be more.

I want to help others, write a book, run a group
Support peers, help them to be whole.
How can I do this when ultimately it's me
That is missing a part of my soul?

My trust was betrayed and my spirit destroyed
and while this is so far in my past,
The effects of believing in someone untrue
Has left angry scars that last.

I'm missing the courage to see my dreams
through
Afraid my judgement is still impaired

Desperately wanting to get that bravery back,
Revert to being she who dares.

I would never abuse the trust of a friend,
I treasure the ones that I've got.
My purpose may still elude me
But Im proud of the things I'm not.

I was asked today "are you happy in life?"
I looked inwards and answered with a smile,
"I'm blessed in more ways I can even describe
and I'll be whole again in just a short while".

Runaway

There was a time in my life that was hopeless.
I lost the ability to smile and have fun.
I was weighed down with worry about my baby
girl.
So I took a breath and started to run.

I ran to escape the sinking feeling
That had taken a hold of my heart.
I ran to shake off the black dog at my heel,
I ran hoping to find my new start.

My mind was declining and straining to leave
Had enough of the future we faced.
My own company indoors was killing me slowly
So I put on my music and raced.

I ran for the grief that was eating me up
I ran from the sorrow that clawed.
I ran from the dark thoughts that lingered within
I ran from the thought I was flawed.

As my feet picked up pace and the music played
And the wind rushed by my weeping eyes
I remembered that I'm chubby and almost 40
And this sudden burst of activity is a surprise.

Running has given me back peace of mind
A chance to reset and to heal.
Running has given me friends for life
A foundation of something so real.

As I see my girls at the finish line
My fatigue and my aches fall away
I run for myself, to keep myself whole
And to make them proud of me every day.

I run to prove my PE teacher wrong.
I'm not asthmatic or inherently slow.
I run to be the best version of me I can be
And to say 'what hell would you know?!'

I run to regulate and I run to revive.
I run to be settled and free
I run to see people to whom I'm not just mum
I run to spend time just as me.

So I may not be fast, may look a right state
I sweat and I pant and I puff
But I always cross that finish line
And say 'Jodie....that was more than enough'

The Clearing

I try not to go too deep into the woods
As deep as I've been before.
But my feet keep moving and before I know
I can no longer see my door.

It's dark in there, so hard to see.
My feet sink in the dirt.
The panic rises up in my throat
My senses on high alert.

Last time I got out, I tried not to look back
Afraid it would pull me back in.
Yet here I am answering its call once again
I'm taking its darkness within.

From in the woods I hear the distant sound
of the voices of those that I know
So close to me yet so far away,
Quieter the further I go.

I spot a beam of hazy light.
A distant symbol of hope.
If I can see that light, no matter how small
I know that I can cope.

The woods, they are not infinite.
I always find my way out.
But while I'm enveloped in their seductive cloak
I will always succumb to doubt.

So please continue to talk while I'm in there
Though you may feel you are talking alone
But when I scramble my way back to the clearing again,
It was your voice that I followed home.

Please Stick

There's a box inside my wardrobe
where my special memories are all kept.
Momentoes from when you entered our world.
The nights I never slept.

The grainy images of a tiny seed.
A bean, a blob of blessed 'please stick'.
A snapshot of reassurance that this time it will
work.
A longing to feel that first kick.

Alongside the images was the band that you
wore
On your impossibly tiny wrist
A feeding cup I tried to use at the start
But if it wasn't a boob you were pissed..

The clip from your cord as gross as that seems
A brush and a single scratch mit.
A cardigan so delicate it fits in my palm
The first item of clothing that fit.

I did the same for your sister, saved a snapshot
in time.
Some treasures to see and to touch.

A selection of items that prove you were loved.
Longed for and wanted so much.

Though I know your many imperfections girls
Your tantrums and your moments of wild.
There's nothing as pure or perfect in this
imperfect world
As the love that you feel for your child.

Vault

The ones that message every day
To say 'have a good one' 'take care'.
The ones you don't see from week to week
But if you needed them they'd be there.

The ones that make you laugh so hard your
cheeks start to ache
The ones that know you inside out.
The ones that hold your secrets like an
impenetrable vault
The ones you simply can't do without.

The ones that dry your tears and pass you tissues
and cake
The ones that make you hold your head up high
The ones that would ride into your battle without
question,
The ones that don't question your why.

The ones that won't let us fall or fail.
The ones that won't let you lose.
Here's to the wonderful friends in our lives.
The family we have the privilege to choose.

This is me

I sometimes wear my bras for weeks,
Turn my knickers inside out.
I sniff milk from the fridge obsessively
and bin it if in doubt.

I brake too late when I drive my car,
I risk three days on zero miles.
My wardrobe is full of clothes I don't wear,
Ones I do sit on the floor in piles.

I avoid answering phone calls the best I can,
I ring back if I must, on my terms.
My house will never be as clean as my Mum's,
I don't believe in invisible germs.

I make plans to do things then let people down,
Unable to say 'it's just not my thing'
I'd avoid large groups of people or even of
friends
Unsure just what to the table I'd bring.

I fill silences even if I just fill it with blah
My mouth works before my brain catches up
I drink more coffee than is good for my health
And I dribble down the side of the cup.

All in all though I'm not a bad sort
I love deeply and I love with no bounds
My children awoke a fighter in me,
A fighter that lasts all the rounds.

If you're lucky enough to be in my circle if
friends,
I'm your cheerleader, your quack and your calm.
I'll only see you once in a very blue moon
But our friendship will suffer no harm.
So that is me Jodie and this is my truth.
Pre-filtered, unedited, me.
But people.....this is the social media era
It's not the me you'll ever see.....

Guppy

You think primary school is where the hard work
stops?
Ha ha ha ha ha ha ha! You wish!
They go from being the big cheese in school
Now in the sea as a guppy fish.

Life's now a messy hash of hormones, fall outs
with drawn talons,
Snidey looks, rumours spread and drama by the
gallons.

Friendships form and friendships break
They fracture, crack and splinter
Cold shoulders paired with icy stares
More harsh than the coldest winter.

They find their feet and bed them in
Personalities form and bloom
The playground wallflower flourishes into the
loudest in the room.

My baby girl becoming a teen is a lesson that
nothing is simple
I miss the pigtails, cuddles, afternoon naps, the
giggles and the dimples.

But it's just one patch in the tapestry
One part of her life's bigger picture.
While it's sugar that makes the pudding sweet
It's the eggs that make it richer.

Tigress

She looked at me.
She looked IN me.
There was no where to hide.
No where to stuff the ugly knots my heart had
homed for years.
Knots my heart had grown around.
Accomodated with resignation that this is how
things are.
Her eyes were innocent yet knowing.
She needed me 100% yet I needed her 110. I felt
like she knew that.
Her cry made me fall apart but then rebuild to
strengthen my armour.
No one would ever hurt her.
How is it that in those vulnerable post birth
moments you can feel so many opposing things?
I was in those moments both raw and healed.
I was broken down.
I was fortified.
Layers of life's gradual build up cracked and fell
away and I was reduced to the most authentic
version of myself I had ever seen.
I was primal.
I was a tigress.

Parchment

Parchment

The crisp air glides into the room as the door
opens.
I breathe deeply and close my eyes to appreciate
the action.
In with a new fresh start, renewed optimism and
hope.
Out with the stale.
Damaging habits, conversations, thoughts and
routines.
Ruminations on all that broke my heart.
Ruminations that when they looked like they
would eventually leave me, I clawed them back
finding comfort in their tight grip.
I'd been lost for a while, calling myself in the
foreboding forest, eventually my voice
becoming a hoarse plea.
I finally heard myself.
I couldn't ignore the desperate cry.
I wrapped my arms around myself so gently,
afraid to tear the fragile parchment that was just
about holding me together.
Fibres so fragile, barely connected.

I realised that the strong hold was coming from
myself.
Fearless, brave and unashamed.
The parchment began to shed, fibre by fibre.
Carried away on the invigorating new breeze.
I became one with myself again.
I'm not afraid anymore.

The Children of 2020

Come on get up! It's back to school!
I shoot my watch a glance
No more last minute log-ons
Or learning in your pants.

The shirt is looking tighter
The starched blue collar creaks
Despite the physical restrictions
It's the most free you've felt in weeks.

You introduce a hairbrush to your mop
You brush your teeth with more vigour
You know yourself that above all else
Your smile today will be bigger.

You still can't believe that you will actually see
your friends in the flesh real soon,
To be in their presence and feel the warmth of
their glow - something quite lacking on Zoom.

You will all have changed in your own ways,
You've been through extraordinary times a
plenty.
You are all bound however by your shared
ordeal

As the children of 2020.

So please let school feel normal real soon
And let's soothe over what you have been
through
But keep close in your heart an appreciation of
life
That will now be ingrained your whole life
through.

Gobshite

Today my child was a gobshite.
A gobshite of the worst kind
The kind that makes you regret life choices so
far
And wonder if you've lost your mind.

Today my child was a gobshite.
And in front of an audience too.
Where is the fun in gobshiting alone,
When an audience will nicely do?

Today my child was a gobshite.
She was vile and stubborn and mean.
To look at her now, it's hard to believe how
She's calmed down from the gobshite she's been.

Today my child was a gobshite.
She embarrassed me in front of my friend.
Could someone who knows send advice my way
As to when the gobshitery will end?

Today my child was a gobshite
The gentle parent in me knows
That the temper we saw was not a character flaw
Just the way that the crucible blows.

Today my child was a gobshite,
But I guess when today is through
This day she was rotten will all be forgotten
After all.... I'm a gobshite too.

Mental Health Awareness Week

It's mental health awareness week
Oh look, here comes another.
An Instagrammer with low self-esteem
Or issues with their Father or Mother.

But sometimes our minds are more complex
than that,
There are issues no categories suit.
An underlying feeling of emptiness
With the odd panic attack to boot.

We all have times where the sun doesn't shine,
and colours seem somehow muted.
You're unable to please anyone, including
yourself,
Your truths all shot down and disputed.

But you my friend, are a work of art
that should ditch this quest for perfection.
The beauty is what comes from the losses and
errors
and the journey from mistake to correction.

While not everyone will appreciate the art that is
you,
because art is as divisive as we are.
You can bet your bottom dollar that at least one
person
Is admiring you from afar.

Collection of Hearts

Would it help if I told you that this feeling
doesn't stay?
There will be a morning when you wake and you
no longer feel this way.
The helplessness, the hopelessness, the need for
some escape
will fade into a life with living.
A life that you can shape.

I've been there loves, I've wrung my hands.
How can I make it stop?
I listed the things I had to live for, with my
children at the top.
But really at the top of that list should have been
a name that I could not see.
My reason for living, for getting well again -
It had to be done for me.

I know you may be parents, siblings and friends,
but you are not a sum of these parts.
You are you in your glorious entirety,
Not just a collection of Hearts.

By all means, draw strength from those that you
love,

They are your retaining wall of hope.
Just know that even without them there,
you are still strong enough to cope.

It's hard to envision a life without stress,
but you will find hints of joy in life again.
You'll look back with such pride that you made
it, you survived,
The days of relentless pain.

Feel those feelings now my friend.
Reach out to others for support and an ear.
When times go dark and you can't find the light,
Just know that life is beautiful with you here.

Bolt from the Blues

This one is for the Fathers and Mothers
that are feeling the 'baby blues'.
A dismissive term if ever there was one
Not the term that most parents would use.

The movies don't depict many difficult births,
they're more horror than a push and a grunt.
They tend not to show the shell-shocked,
traumatised Mum,
that's been torn from front to back.

The nights in which the world's asleep
while you're painstakingly shushing and feeding.
"Ah those magic times of your baby at your
breast".
Yeah magic mate. My nipples are bleeding.

I love my babies with all that I am,
despite all the stretches and tears.
Please let's normalise things like intrusive
thoughts
of dropping your baby down the stairs.

It's normal to worry this stuff may take place
while you adapt to a love so profound.

A love that evolves around an exhaustion so
severe,
You feel trampled into the ground.

Go chat to your GP if these blues feel more
than the effect of recurrent all nighters.
Post-natal depression can be treated well whilst
we navigate raising these blighters.

My loves, all you can do is to try your best,
dish out that love even when the going gets
tough.
No matter how many vegetables they eat,
they'll be embarrassed by you soon enough.

Holes

You tell her that her walk is weird.
'So weird!' your shadow chimes.

Her walk to me is what it should be at 13.
A little unsure, awkward, uncertain, clumsy.
I remember the first tentative steps.
Arms outstretched - mouth wide open in
disbelief.

You tell her she is fat.
You send her pictures of herself with her
perceived flaws circled.

Her curves are perfection.
Not in need of any correction.
Standing on the precipice of womanhood with a
furtive gaze back occasionally to the child that is
left behind a little more every day.

Her skin as soft as the day she was born,
when I delicately stroked her face
and touched her nose to check that she was real.

My miracle gift and God what a gift!
She was the gift of life but also

she was the gift of my life.

You will never see what I do
or feel for her what I do
you bore holes in her to an audience
and drill more and more if you're inclined to

but I see you.

Because under those clothes are the gaping holes
that were caused in you by someone that should
know better
than to idly stand by watching as your clothes
get wetter.

Hurt people hurt people
and whilst I believe that to be true,
as a Mother I simply cannot stand by
and observe this damage to her that you do.

One day you'll bore too many, too big
and they will be too wide to plug.
My beautiful gift will just lie down defeated
in the pit of her despair that you dug.

Your holes will remain,
and your own soul still drain.
You'll have just passed on your pain
in an attempt to make yourself whole.

Gratitude

On a day when we celebrate gratitude,
It's a valuable chance to reflect
Not just the usual churned out platitudes
what we all may have come to expect.

We're all grateful for family and friends
that enhance our everyday lives.
The children that make us fulfilled and
complete,
the dedicated Husbands and Wives.

But you know what else I'm grateful for?
A life map of multi terrains.
Enjoying the smooth easy paths we may walk as
well as those that cause weariness and pains.

I'm grateful for those that tried to break me
down,
because you fortified my internal armour.
I learned to regulate in the face of chaos
and respond to it more dignified.........calmer.

I'm grateful for the opportunity to experience
bad hair,
My weird Barbie arc was humbling for sure.

Of course I harped on that it empowered me and
all that while really crying daily in shame behind
a closed door.

I'm grateful for Facebook memories.
The daily reminder of what's gone before.
The baby pics I love to recall and wow! How
they've grown!
Cringe statuses and fringe mistakes galore.

I am genuinely one lucky lady though,
because I am here, breathing, right now.
If we didn't have times where we test our resolve
then we may never really learn how.

At the time these trials are unpleasant,
unrelenting
and such lessons are concealed by the weight.
Hindsight is truly a wonderful thing
though its arrival can sometimes feel late.

Your gratitude may not come on gratitude day
but rather in a quiet moment in time.
When you can think "I'm so glad that cloud has
now passed.,
but this lesson - this lesson here is mine".

The Emotional Support Pumpkin

It was October 2022 and I made a huge mistake.
One so catastrophic - one I definitely won't
remake.

I was doing the big shop in Lidl
 and was in the veggie aisle,
when I spotted a miniature pumpkin so cute
I just couldn't help but smile!

I thought how Esme would love this too,
It could sit in our window for Halloween.
When I brought it home her eyes lit up
in a way I have never seen.

"I'm calling her Nellie" She declared
after my Grandma that sadly passed.
Nellie went from miniature squash
to a family member real fast.

She was cuddled over and over and
carried faithfully everywhere.
Esme even bathed with Nellie,
washing her down with care.

Halloween came and went again
yet Nellie was still going strong.
I'd say it was around mid December that things
really started to go wrong.

Nellie became soft around the edges,
I know - it happens to us all,
but she started to smell like a teacher's breath
and look like a shriveled ball.

I'd hold my breath when Nellie was close,
Stomach turning at her decomposition.
When I bought her all those weeks ago, I never
foresaw being in this position.

We tried putting her in the freezer at night,
to slow her inevitable demise
but sadly by New Year she was far too gone
I explained as Esme sadly cries.

We held a funeral in the garden,
placing her under a plastic pot.
Esme's heart broke as she said her goodbyes
To little Nellie who was now a slushy pile of rot.

"I don't ever want another pumpkin mum"
She said to my palpable relief.
I had no idea my whimsical buy
would cause a tsunami of grief.

She checked on Nellie recently
who is a pile of seeds in her grave.
Her emotional support pumpkin was so very
loved
and still is - in her plastic cave.

Beware these thoughtless purchases!
They're more dangerous than you think.
You may wake up one morning to a squash
having a bubble bath in your sink.

Yes Please!

This one's for the people pleasers,
the ones that never say no.
If you metaphorically beat us continuously,
we would politely smile with every blow.

"I'd love to do this" I may offer out loud.
"but oh, you'd rather go there?"
"Then let's go there! A much better idea!"
"No I don't mind - I don't care!"

Can I give you a lift? Of course I can!
12 miles isn't out of my way.
My dinner looks good? Well here you go,
I'm watching my weight anyway.

Not all people pleasing is so overt.
Some sacrifices more subtle to detect.
Like changing your ways gradually over time
Becoming someone they're less likely to reject.

I may try to speak more quietly, in a more
hushed tone
as I can 'whisper over seven fields' it's said.
I may think twice before joining a conversation
and practice my part in my head.

Fellow people pleasers, I'd love to say
there's a time when you will just stop.
Prioritise yourself and your own needs
making sure for once you come out on top.

I'm yet to find this Nirvana though and
behaviours will continue until
I start to stop putting acceptance as more
important than
championing my own free will.

There's nothing wrong with being 'nice'
so long as it isn't misplaced.
Giving should be a two way street
on which decency and humanity is based.

One day we will be our own best advocate,
but until that idyllic day arrives
We'll keep offering our backs for target practice
then offering to clean the knives.